To Begin:

A JOURNEY IN SELF LOVE AND HEALING

SAKINA IBRAHIM

RESOURCE *Publications* • Eugene, Oregon

TO BEGIN
A Journey in Self-Love and Healing

Wipf & Stock
An Imprint of Wipf and Stock Publishers
199 W. 8th Ave., Suite 3
Eugene, OR 97401

www.wipfandstock.com

PAPERBACK ISBN: 978-1-6667-3166-8
HARDCOVER ISBN: 978-1-6667-2436-3
EBOOK ISBN: 978-1-6667-2437-0

Edited by Tonya C. Johnson & Jhani Randawa—www.jfkrandhawa.com
Formated by Michael Davie—www.grimhousepub.com

For the women determined to heal and all survivors and victims of domestic violence.

CONTENTS

Thank you to my beautiful mother Caroline, Grandmother Mattie, Aunt Nicki, Jaedyn, my Brother Khalid, Khai, Lisa, Nate and Bobby. I do everything for you all. "Family Over Everything." Thank you to my fur-babies; Miracle, Magic, and Chocolate. You bring me joy each day. Thank you to all my beautiful soul sista girlfriends for having my back and holding me up when my head has been down. To my friend and Editor, Jhawi and her wonderful parents, Susan and Manjeet, your compassion and support has fueled my ability to soar while away from my family. To Adil and Leslie, thank you for keeping it real and holding me accountable to honoring my life. Thank you to my agents, publisher, and team of accountability partners. I acknowledge all of my teachers, mentors, supporters and those who have ever supported and watered the seeds of Sakina Ibrahim.

Introduction

I t is never easy to begin. We often have dreams and ideas, things we need to accomplish in our personal and spiritual life that are difficult to get off the ground. Life forces you to grow and step into your destiny by allowing us to experience pain. That pain has to be released through our relationships with people. I believe all life elements work together as an energy source that pulsates from our being and drives us to nurture a relationship with the highest source of love and energy. Many people call this energy; I am referring to God.

There are so many places along my self-love journey where I could begin, but I want to start with one of the most recent pain experiences: my first heartbreak, after a brutal end to a long term relationship. I realized the relationship was not the only thing that ended—I also had to break up with the old version of myself.

It was February 1st, the month of love, ironically. A time where people are excited about celebrating Valentine's Day or what my ex-boyfriend and I called black love day. I had already begun to pack my items. I did not know where I was going, but I knew I had to move out. I had not been sleeping and I felt heavy and depressed whenever I was home. I had gained weight; I just was not happy anymore.

My ex-boyfriend and I met when I was in undergrad in Philadelphia. He was a well-known figure in the city and I was an overly ambitious college student who loved going out dancing. We connected through dancing and it became something we enjoyed doing together. He was supportive and taught me a lot about life and spirituality. He introduced me to vegetarian books and my favorite author, Eckhart Tole. We took trips to Miami and would have the best time on jet skis, eating at the most beautiful restaurants, dancing all night into the morning at clubs, and falling asleep on the beach, only to wake up and do it all over again. We indeed had a good time together.

Our relationship came to a few crossroads, the first being when I decided to move to California. Actually, on our first date, I told him I didn't want to get involved with him because I was moving to California. His response was, "I'll marry you and move you to California." After undergrad, I made my move across the country and he didn't come. He was not ready. We went through the horrors that come with long-distance relationships: cheating, miscommunication, spending money on trips to see each other. Deep down, I felt like this was the end of the relationship until I got a call that he had been in a bad accident, leaving him paraplegic, amongst other injuries.

It was a scary experience, but I was by his side through it all. I left California and moved to New York, where he relocated and signed up to be there through what I knew was a long road to recovery. I did what I thought was the right thing and I did what I knew no other woman would do. I sacrificed my life and goals for love. I tried to do my best to stay centered on who I was, but I was in my twenties and still discovering that version of myself.

I often prayed and meditated. My long walks with my dogs would lead me to the top of a hill where I would sit and talk to God.

I started to feel like I did not have a life of my own. My career was not where I wanted it to be. Although I did have some success with my first book, workshops, and speaking engagements, I just felt like I could not get my feet off the ground. I felt like the only thing that would help me to feel secure in this relationship was marriage. I told him I wanted to get married. I told him I would no longer "play house" without an engagement and clarity about "what we were doing."

About a year later, after the ultimatum, I jumped up from a dream. In this dream, I heard a voice. The voice said, "It's time to go, you've done your part." It was time to leave this relationship. It was officially the beginning of the end of the only romantic-love partnership I had ever known. I kept praying and meditating on the outcome I wanted. I wanted a new apartment for myself and my dogs, and I wanted a new life. I didn't know what a life without him would look like, but I was willing to try. I started saving money and sharing my plans with him so he would not be taken by surprise when he came home, and my things were gone. I think deep down, he didn't believe I was going anywhere. My closet was empty, and I felt the same way. I did not have anywhere to go. I knew that preparing and setting my intentions to go would open the way.

One night I fell asleep on the sofa, which never happens. I woke up the next morning and went to the gym. On my way back home I saw him, hugged him, and felt this would be the last time I would ever see him.

Shortly after, a text had come through from a girl from craigslist who needed to rent her apartment. When I went to see the apartment, she gave me the keys and said, "I have a flight to catch; move in when you want and send me the deposit when you get it." I called a friend to help me load the car, and by 3 pm that same day, I was gone. It was over. I lay on the floor of the new apartment and cried.

Later, I got a call from a friend who was also a spiritual advisor. She told me to get a Bible and read Psalm 91. I had not read the Bible in about five years, but I listened. I drove to Barnes and Nobles and read that scripture, which made me feel a sense of protection and comfort.

I knew he would be worried and that his heart would be crushed, but I also knew I had to be obedient and choose my happiness. I had to choose my own life. My life was brought down to the ground. It was at this point, after walking out of the apartment I shared with my partner and being flooded with a range of emotions that I realized I was at a crossroad in my life. I knew one thing: everything that was lost would be restored. I called my mom to come to town to help me center because I was undoubtedly a mess emotionally and struggled to keep my thoughts and professional life together.

I started the healing myself by doing a detox and going plant-based; this helped me lift my vibration. I was sleeping better, I started losing weight, and became happier. I was doing yoga, and I felt like I was on the road to creating a beautiful single life. Simultaneously, I acted out my pain in irresponsible ways, like partying hard and intoxicating myself to numb out. It was a tug of war between feeling the pain, the loss, and trying to numb it out by pretending to have the time of my life at nightclubs. I had a good time, but I knew this was not the woman I wanted to be. I wanted to heal truly. When I could finally hear myself above the tug-of-war struggle, I started to walk at the beach and committed to being in nature every day. I prayed every day. I started going to spas and reading books about self-care and love. Still, daily I felt tormented by the past. I felt hated by his family and afraid of what people were going to think of me. "She left a man in a wheelchair; how could she?" The truth I was discovering for myself was that I loved, supported, and took care of a man in a wheel-chair for five years. When I was no longer happy, I chose to take care of myself.

I had to decide to get over it eventually! I turned off all the lights in my room, cried hard and loud, and told myself when I wake up in the morning, I am done grieving! I am deciding to move forward and no longer live in the past, and that is precisely what began to happen!

I told myself I would know the healing had begun when I could laugh about the events that had taken place; when I could laugh at my insanity and the insanity of others.

That moment has come, and now I am open to sharing part of my learning journey to love myself.

CHAPTER
1
Always Find The Light

Most people think standing in the light is an illuminating process, that you feel all of this love and greatness from God: that you can float, at least I did. However, to become light or return to the light, you must face some darkness. You must face some ugly parts of yourself. Many of us have been conditioned to think we are less than worthy, particularly when we re-encounter parts of ourselves that have experienced trauma, heartbreak, loss and grief. Yet, it is these life circumstances that force us into our healing and our life purpose. Life has its ways of bringing us so low down our only choice is to look inward and upward.

This part of becoming enlightened and self-discovery is not famous. It does not stand on stage and motivate or inspire people. It does not have millions of views and likes. This part of enlightenment comes out when no one else is there but you, when you are all alone facing the darkest part of your being. As you are face to face with your demons, you have a choice to evolve or continue to live in the dysfunctions of your public persona and ego. We always have a choice, which is why we face the same obstacles multiple times. Each encounter is a test presenting us with the opportunity to make a different choice.

One of the first life events that brought me to this place was the death of my Uncle Carl. If you have read my first book, Big Words to Little Me: Advice to the Younger Self, you may know that Carl was the victim of gang violence, leaving him blind, mute, and paralyzed. He had limited physical ability, but his presence and spirit were strong and unforgettable. The circumstances of his life taught me early the power of empathy and compassion.

It was three days after my 26th birthday, and I had just left the Macy's Flower Show in Time Square with my partner. I was getting calls from home all day but was having trouble connecting to my family members. Finally, I was able to communicate with my mother, who said: "You need to get home, it's Carl." I interrupted her by asking, "Is Carl dead?" She said, "Just get home!" I screamed at the top of my lungs and curled over onto the floor. I just kept crying. I did not know the sound of horror and pain lived in me in that capacity. With my body and the phone dropped to the floor, I was present enough to say to myself, "this is grief, this is what grief feels like, this is what loss feels like, feel it Sakina."

There weren't any more buses or trains going back to Massachusetts that night, so I ended up taking a $400 cab ride from New York to Massachusetts. When I walked into the private room where the hospital holds families awaiting bad news, about fifteen of my family members gathered. I hugged everyone, then sat on my grandmother's lap and rubbed her head.

My grandmother was Carl's primary caregiver, and in this role, she sacrificed herself and loved him unconditionally. I watched her work from 11 pm to 7 am as a nurse, then come home to care for her disabled son for the remainder of the day. She was always dedicated to his well-being, his recovery, and making sure he felt deeply loved. From this cloth, I am cut. I honor her, my mother, and my aunt in the deepest ways; for they taught me what I know about being of service and giving selflessly. We know giving when there is nothing to be returned, nothing but an inner fulfillment in knowing that we have done our part to love.

In the hospital waiting room, the doctors had told us there was nothing they could do. Because Carl already experienced severe brain damage from the initial accident when a gang attacked him, this time, his brain would not be able to recover. They leaned towards pulling the plug and wanted our permission to do it before the official brain dead tests were complete. The room was still with fear and trauma.

Looking around the room, I realized no one was going to speak, so I said: "In the spirit of my grandfather, you do everything you can to keep him here as long as you can. We are a people of faith, and we do not give up. We will pray." We all stood up, held hands, and my little cousin led us in a powerful Pentecostal prayer. There was not a dry eye in the room, and even the doctor teared up. I believe that was his first experience feeling the energy of the holy spirit in the hospital. The prayer brought peace into the room and much unity in my family was created. We believed God could do all things, but I think we all knew we were in the beginning phases of saying goodbye to our beloved, Anthony Carl Rosemond.

We all took turns talking to Carl, massaging his feet, playing his favorite rappers, including Wu-Tang Clan and Method Man. At one moment, when no one was in the room, I saw his hands twitching. I could not tell if he was fighting to stay or making his exit. I opened his eyelids and they looked soul-less. Although he was blind, his eyes always had life, curiosity, and joy in them. This time there was no life. I never told anyone this: I could see his soul was gone. Maybe even lingering; although his body was still there, he was not with us anymore. He laid there, his face swelling from internal bleeding. The family was around him sharing their final words.

Grama said something along the lines of, "You were the world's most beautiful baby. No one should have done this to you. I love you, but it is time."

We all shared our unique way of letting him know we loved him and that we knew the power of the spirit. His spirit would live on. Energy does not die; it only transforms. Some of us shared feelings of resentment from his condition, feeling like it required us to be loved less as children and that we had to sacrifice ourselves. Everything had revolved around Carl for most of our lives. It was time to admit that his trauma had affected us. We hadn't been allowed the opportunity to heal while pushing through violence and its normalization—the thread of my family's experience is part of the cultural braid of so many black families' experiences. Our lives do not exist without fear and violence. Black families have been trapped in the tornado of violence since placing their feet on American plantations.

Saying goodbye to Carl meant we were departing from parts of ourselves. We would have to transform the narrative about our lives and our identity as a family. We had a choice, to hold on to the inner narrative of the past pain or forgive and create a new story that would bring peace and inner freedom. I would start my journey by going to therapy.

The doctor came in the room and did the final brain dead test. We held onto each other and held our breath as they told us, "He is gone, he has been gone." Death had occurred. The loss was in full effect, tears rolling, screams from the hallways echoing.

I remember going into the waiting room and praying for his soul and his happiness. On the way, I saw my aunt in the hallway, angry and crying, being held down by my cousin who was screaming, "Jesus come help us!" The chaos and grief felt so out of control, so impossible to control. I remember walking down the hall and my body giving out. I fell and kept saying, "My uncle is dead. He is gone." I was just trying to understand how it happened so fast. In that moment, how had my life been moving so fast and so slowly at the same time?

Seeing and feeling all of this made me realize this is the price we pay when we love, knowing we must let go. That is real love. It is fully surrendering to its presence beyond form. Its presence is like air—you cannot see it, but it is there. You feel it, and because you feel, that is what sustains you. Life is nothing without love, and love is nothing without loss. This experience was like a whisper from God, saying, "Love is knowing I am there without form."

We experienced the flow of funeral planning, guilt, and anger. Shortly before Carl passed, I started to work with a local film company on documenting his story and how trauma and violence affect families over generations. The most interesting part of the documentary is when the interviewer asked Carl if he forgave his attackers. With conviction, he stated NO. I judged him for his truth, and now I respect his truth. I understand it was his soul journey to learn life lessons through his circumstances and to give lessons to those around us. We all chose a path. Every choice allows the path to unfold in many directions.

I often wonder when his soul was transitioning if he had forgiven. I wonder if you can transition into the after-life without forgiveness. I do not know the answers, I wonder. I do know there is an inner peace that comes with the words, "I forgive you." I often imagine him being at peace, smiling, free from the captivity of his body, the violence, and the pain and frustration.

Carl's life taught me the most beautiful lessons about deep forgiveness and compassion. His death taught me grief and pain are the other sides of love. Both are something you have to surrender to; it is part of the beauty of life. Life is full of phases; watching something grow, then die and grow again, just like flowers in a garden. We exist in the flower of life, our time here on this earth is brief. We need to enjoy it and laugh more often. We need to take responsibility for our experiences and know that it is no one else's responsibility to take care of us. We must take on the truth of knowing we are all connected and approach our relationships with the same grace we would want to receive.

The more we understand and appreciate life's value and beauty, the more we appreciate the true reality that death is part of the cycle. Therefore, I find it so important to live fully. We know how short life is. We have seen people, even children, gunned down by police and drive-by shootings. We have witnessed the seconds it takes for a person's precious life to be gone. Many people do not get to experience the blessing of saying goodbye. The more willing we are to live and value what we have while we are here, the more we can respect life phases. One of my favorite quotes shared by a dance mentor, Donald McKaye is, "Life and death are one, even as the river and sea are one" – Khalil Gibron.

This loss required us to begin to create a new normal, missing a member of our tribe. The lesson I was starting to learn was to begin surrendering to what I thought I knew about life. I found it liberating to admit to myself, "I don't know anything," I need to do some unlearning and approach the real meaning of life differently. I needed to let go, to pray for clarity, and begin a new journey of appreciating who I was. It was as if when life gives you pain, it is saying here is a new chance.

CHAPTER

2

Holding On Too Tight

We hold so much in, we hold in anger and frustration, we hold in love and we hold in fear. We have to learn to tell the truth and let it go. Maybe sometimes that does not feel comfortable or safe and it doesn't provide a relaxing feeling. Maybe it is scary and rocks your world the way an earthquake would, but if we were to release, maybe we would feel a little lighter and life would be easier to carry on.

The words "carry on" have powerful energy behind them. This phrase may serve as a mantra to stay present. You know the times when you are about to lose your temper and are having trouble staying present because your thoughts are wandering about something that hasn't and probably will never happen? Try saying the words carry on to bring you back into the present moment.

Life has its earthquakes and these moments are compelling us to shake off what no longer serves us. Shake off excess energy. We do not have to judge it or make it right or wrong, we just have to be with it and let it pass.

We have to allow it to carry on until it is no longer a thought or action with power or influence over us. This takes time and it is a practice.

Sometimes we are holding too tight to jobs, relationships, and old ideas that no longer serve us. Fear is only there as a form or tool through which we grow and become aware. Fear is there as a shadow to show us in which direction we need to grow next.

For many years I was afraid to build a relationship with my father. You see, it is complicated because he's in prison. He's been there for most of my life. He gets to call me once a week for 15 minutes. I wrote to him for the first time when I was 27 years old. We wrote letters for a while and eventually, I trusted him enough to call. This trust was necessary because he has a reputation for doing some horrible things when he was in the streets. He was abusive to my mother and sold drugs. He even tried to kidnap my brother and me from my mother. Eventually, he was charged with murder and sentenced to 25 years to life in prison.

It hurts that my father was not there to raise me or positively contribute to my life; to teach me to be loved by a man. I had to learn it was safe enough to surrender to love. Many women maintain the perspective that they do not need a man to be strong Black women. We don't maintain these perspectives because we want to, but because we have to survive and we have to protect ourselves. To be a strong Black woman, we must also learn to allow ourselves to be vulnerable. Trust me, this is not easy in a white supremacist patriarchal world. Our daily experience as Black women is affected by various emotional, mental, and sometimes physical acts of violence from the reinforcement of Anti-Black and anti-woman values and systems. In the world, as we know it, it is very difficult to feel physically and emotionally safe enough to surrender and trust that if we let go, we will be safe and protected. I think we must permit ourselves to create a new reality and no longer look to the outside world to make us feel seen and loved. We have to permit ourselves to be free enough to love ourselves.

Black women are socialized with images from the media and community that relate to a lack of connection, protection, and commitment from male counterparts, including our fathers. The question that is programmed in our minds when fathers aren't there for their little girls or when they break their promises to us is, "Doesn't he want me, and doesn't he love me?" This narrative becomes a lurking shadow in many of our relationships until we can unlearn it. I was not even aware of this inner narrative until a man told me he felt rejected by my resistance to allow him to show up and lead as a partner in my life. I wanted to do everything myself. I wanted to be in complete control all the time and I was afraid that it would make me weak if I relied on a man. That something was being taken from me. Honestly, where was I supposed to learn how to rely on or trust a man? Where was I supposed to learn that I was respected, honored, and protected by a man? When our fathers are not there, this is what happens. A breakdown in our perception and expectations in relationships, dysfunctional cycles that keep us from having the families and lives we truly deserve.

Another shadow that remained with me was the feeling that it was much safer for me to expect disappointment from a man than to expect my needs to be met. A friend helped me become aware of this ingrained lesson by telling me, "We usually get what we expect." Once I changed my expectations, my relationships also began to change.

I have grown to become a compassionate listener with my father and to see him as a man who made mistakes. We live in a world that profits off the mistakes of black men. Suppose people knew the inhumane conditions of the penitentiary system and understood what happens inside of it. In that case, I am certain any person with a soul would agree prisons should not exist as they do in America. I recall my father saying, "We are animals here, we are not human beings, nor can we conduct ourselves as such. Having love and compassion in prison will get me killed." This statement let me know that prison is the darkest place on earth and should not be glamorized.

My father did not have a close relationship with his children and that is one of his biggest regrets. Another regret is that his decisions truly led him one of his biggest regrets. Another regret is that his decisions truly led him to throw his life away. Prison and gang culture are glamorized in the media and entertainment industries. Yet, we rarely see the experiences of the families and children who also become imprisoned. The families are held captive psychologically and emotionally by the absent parent or loved one.

The first attempts talking on the phone with my father were really difficult. It was hard to find a way to communicate that did not infantilize me while also making him feel empowered in very disempowering circumstances. He overshared his relationship with my mom in his letters, and I often found myself saying that he was a crazy-ass man! I realize now that calling him crazy is a simple way to dismiss his trauma and his experiences as a Black man that led him to make bad decisions. My father's father was also in prison and died just a few days after being released from unattended heart issues, so my father grew up in the same circumstances as I did: a broken family affected by the prison system.

As much as I wanted to love my father, I also felt the need to judge him. It took some time until I decided to look at him from a spiritual lens and release my guilt and anger. I had to accept that he chose his life lessons and that he had to walk his path and transform himself. Eventually, we found common ground and I can open my heart and see him with respect and dignity. I had to remove the anger and see both of us through the lens of compassion to move forward.

One of my spiritual advisors told me that we choose our parents for the lessons we need to learn and the tools we need in this lifetime, which aligns with the idea that we sign up for our soul growth lessons. My parents chose each other, and I chose them. Healing my relationship with my father has allowed me to heal from many issues with my male relationships and expectations of men. Some women hold men to an unrealistic standard, thinking that we will be whole or wholly happy if we have a man or are in a relationship. Having a man only brings out that which has not been healed yet. Healing with my father has allowed me to witness men's humanity; to realize they have pain, trauma, and healing to be done too. Previously, I saw all men as heroes that were going to save us girls from our problems. WRONG! WRONG! WRONG! We, together as the Yin and Yang, are here to balance each other and to balance the world. A balanced and successful relationship with yourself and your male partner can only happen if you are ready to face yourself and let go of the ideas and notions that no longer serve you. "Let go, everything will fall into place."

CHAPTER

3

Sex It Away

L ove is so complicated. Many of my friends have been struggling deeply in their love relationships. Being heartbroken and trying to piece together ways to fill the void of love in their lives. I, too, am one of those women. I always measured my worth and beauty based on whether a man wanted, needed, or loved me. I think most of us girls are taught this behavior at a young age. I remember my first crush, Ralphel. We called him Ralphy—a Puerto Rican boy with a birthmark on his face that was just so cute to me. He did not like me, but I would write him notes to circle yes or no if he liked me every day. I remember the day I just knew he was going to change his mind. I sent my best friend, Amanda, to give him my note. He took the note and started walking towards the trash. I said to myself, "He's gonna throw it away," and he sure did. I was crushed! My little heart was so hurt that he did not even have the decency to circle no and give me an answer!

This early experience with Ralphy sent me a little brain code that said when you share your feelings, your requests from men will not be answered, and you will get hurt when you share how you feel. Even more, you feel as though if you tell the truth you will be silenced, so you don't say anything. Do not tell the partner you love that you love them, or when your feelings are hurt, do not be vulnerable! Keep it all inside and be strong. Cry when nobody's watching. Growing up, we experience many phases in our dynamic with men that leave us with messages that affect our future relationships with ourselves and others. The rejection I have faced put me in a pattern of wanting a specific kind of guy who did not want me back. It took a lot of time and maturity to accept that I was attracting a certain relationship, connecting to that inner dialogue that says, "daddy doesn't want to be here." Which energetically manifests into, "my man doesn't want me, he doesn't want to be here."

I had a major aha moment in my relationship where I had to be shown by my partner a series of examples on how he wants to be in my life and in my presence. Although the actions were there, my perception was limited. Our inner messages can be so deeply coded we can be in the presence of that which we desire and still project our past trauma onto our blessings. It is taking me many hours of internal work to release and reprogram my mind and my life. First, simply becoming aware of what the message is, recognizing how it shows up in my thoughts and actions, then affirming the experience I do want to have. "I enjoy having a partner who is present and loving with me." I say things like this over and over again. Embedding it into a sensation, feeling, and belief. I believe God wants good for us, so any thought or thing that is not good has to be released. Jeremiah 29:11 says, "For I know the plans I have for you," declares the LORD, "plans to prosper you and not to harm you, plans to give you hope and a future." This is telling us God's intentions for us. We just have to believe that it is true and that we are worthy of goodness.

Intimacy

We often think intimacy is only sexual. However, intimacy can also be emotional and spiritual bonding. Intimacy is a relationship that should be cutivated throughout our lives from the inside out. Our elders should be teaching us how to be intimate and carry ourselves with grace instead of frowning upon what is looked at as promiscuous behavior or what you might hear as "being fast." When we don't know what to do with our sexual energy, it will most likely get misplaced and misused–leaving multiple generations of early pregnancy, low- self-esteem, and broken relationships.

Men are not taught how to be intimate or how to control their sexual energy either. Conversations only go as deep as, "use a condom" or "don't get anyone pregnant." What if there were deeper conversations about how to embrace the natural aspects of growing into our womanhood? What if we had a safe space to express our sexual energy. As women, we have to create that space for ourselves and shift the sexualization of our bodies and our sexual energy. Once the male gaze comes upon our bodies, our sexual and sensual nature no longer feels sacred and spiritual. It feels like we have to protect ourselves from the idea that a man who looks at us wants to have sex with us. We must protect ourselves from the possibility of sexual assault.

Men need to evolve past primal instincts, respect the female body, and the woman's intimate nature. I am trying to say that women should feel safe in their sexuality and sensuality. It is part of our gift to life.

Sexual trauma and abuse are way too common. I know so many women who have experienced someone touching them inappropriately. Families know about it, but often do not know how to address it because they went through it too. There are generations of women (and men) who were not kept safe and did not have access to the proper resources to heal past the trauma. Childhood sexual abuse leaves deep and difficult wounds to heal because of the shame and embarrassment. Research has shown those who have experienced sexual abuse often experience higher levels of depression, guilt, shame, self-blame, eating disorders, somatic concerns, anxiety, dissociative patterns, repression, denial, sexual problems, and relationship problems.

It wasn't until later in life, when I embarked on true intimacy and true love, that I became aware of how being touched inappropriately affected me emotionally and tarnished my perception of men. I know many women reading this book may be able to identify. I want to share that you do not have to go through the journey of looking into that closet of hidden pain alone. Get to therapy now! Take your power back and comfort the child who did not have a voice, power, or control. As an adult, you can heal and reclaim what was stolen from you. It takes time, but you will heal and overcome the results of that trauma in your life.

We have to be more mindful of who we let into our wombs and energetic vortexes. Our vaginas are a portal to life, literally the channel that brings forth life. We must be responsible for who we allow having access to that space. I know today, sex is no big deal. Our language and behavior around sex are so casual. It was not until I was well into my adulthood and deep in my spiritual journey that I was taught the secrets of sexual intercourse and what is happening on an energetic and soul level. After understanding how deep it is, I truly had regrets for all the partners I have had.

Sex is sacred for a reason. Our spirits should not be intertwined with anyone besides our married partners. I have tried to do it my way and make excuses that align with what the world says is okay. Honestly, there is no reward in having sex outside of marriage. On a soul level, you pray at a high price.

It is not just you and the person; it is you, your partner, and God. Your souls merge, and a soul tie is created. Every thrust is energy coming into your soul. That is why so many people end up blinded by who they really are after they sleep with them. The energy has been bound together. That is why many women go crazy over men and end up messing their lives up because of a man who was not ready, nor interested in taking on any responsibility; or for a man who was wrong for them in the first place. We often embark on sexual relationships without even knowing the person. Sometimes women can feel like something has been taken from them when a guy stops calling or demonstrates a lack of interest after having sex with them. It hurts! We do not always understand why it hurts, but it just does. Even if we pretend it does not. Not getting our emotional needs met in addition to our physical needs is not fulfilling.

Men are taught they can screw you and not get attached, but our vaginas have a direct connection to the heart. Even if we think we are just hooking up and not getting attached, the heart does not know the difference. The heart longs for love, while the body longs for bliss and pleasure. After so many years of empty sex, you begin to feel empty inside. You begin to have a hard time recognizing true love. You begin to want the pleasure over and over again. You have developed a pattern of getting this love, avoiding getting hurt and keeping the true love that is praying for you at a distance because you are out of alignment.

We fall into patterns of seeking love from a man instead of seeking love from the source; it comes from God. That is the only source that can truly fulfill us. Why would we think that a flawed human being could complete us? We are trying to create a synthetic version of love with broken men, leaving our future daughters and ourselves in a cycle of low expectations and a lack of fulfillment in relationships.

I made a risky choice to stop having sex and tell the men I was dating or who wanted to date me that I was not having sex until I was in a committed relationship; it has done wonders for me. I generally attract plenty of male attention with my calm and confident nature, but when I drop the news and layout the standards I have, they scramble, stutter, and try to pretend it is cool and that sex is not the main motive. I loved myself enough to create some standards that changed my life and helped to weed out the jokers and accept a partner who was serious about me and co-creating a life together.

The desire to keep my legs closed and stop having sex came during meditation. It was a truly clear download from God concerning what I needed to do to advance to my next level. As I continued to grow spiritually and experience divine love and bliss from God, I no longer had the desire to seek validation from people or material things. I discovered the true essence of love and was no longer interested in the knockoff versions that were deceitful. When you begin to discover yourself and the greatness that you were created from, nothing in society and no man, can convince you that you should give ALL of yourself to them without feeling love and without knowing the true intentions of their soul.

Now, as I discover myself in relationships I form them based on true connection and purpose—not just on sexual pleasure or drunken-love. This has become such a liberating practice.

In my journey of building friendships and relationships with men, I am learning men have not learned how to treat the heart responsibly. Not much about their socialization allows them to learn the process of being vulnerable and tender with their feelings, let alone to another. Crying has always been seen as weak. We have all heard the saying, "boys don't cry."

I have been learning that men feel; it is just that many are not trained in expressing it. Their emotional IQ might be lower, but they can do the work. A male friend told me most men have low self-esteem and have not been taught to love themselves. With this in mind, I wonder why we as women give so much credit to a being that still has to learn to love himself and develop emotional intelligence too. We are all out here looking in the wrong places with little guidance. No wonder my girls and I are devastated by disappointments caused by men. We have expectations of each other that are not realistic. We assume the other person knows how to express their feelings, needs, or wants–but what if they do not? That is the reason healing and mental health are so important. I knew addressing mental and emotional health was an important requirement for me when manifesting a partner. I knew I wanted someone who was on his healing and wellness path. That would be the only way it would work; how could I be the only one meditating and in therapy?

I am discovering love because we have to unlearn everything, selecting what we want to keep that is grounded in universal truth and not in Disney romance. When I discovered Disney romance wasn't real, I felt so deceived. I felt like we had been taught so many lies, and everyone knew they were lies, except for women. We must wake up and realize that only we can create the relationships and partnerships we desire from the inside out. We truly have to learn compassion for ourselves and empathy for others . The more empathy I have, the less angry I can be, and the freer I am. I am not saying allow anyone to walk all over you–I am saying, ask questions that will help clarify and not reinforce false expectations. I am saying, believe someone's actions, just like I should have believed that Ralphy did not like me when he did not answer my note the first time, instead of asking over and over again.

Sometimes you will have to sit through the pain of being alone to manifest the greatness of what you deserve, which is the best. Relationships require work and personal change. The best relationship to establish is the one with yourself. You can only give what you have for yourself.

I have heard this many times in my life before I got it. My friends and I went to see this Buddhist monk prophet in Texas in 2020, around the time the Covid 19 pandemic hit. He said many profound things, but one of the things I gained from his stories was when he talked about his grandmother laughing at him when he was going to get married to a girl. She told him something along the lines of how can you get married when you don't love yourself, that is your first marriage. Let's take a moment to take that in. Your first marriage, union, contract, and expression of commitment is to yourself. When that is established, you can then create and shape what your marriage looks like, where the boundaries are, and how you will create your life. When you are full, you do not expect your partner to make you happy. You are aware that you make yourself happy, and someone gets to share that experience with you.

Take your time falling in love and having a love affair with you. To have the best, you have to become your best. I am drawn to Ephesians 4:2, "Be completely humble and gentle; be patient, bearing with one another in love." This encourages me to be gentle and kind to myself and others in the process of discovering love. I am learning to feel what there is to feel and surrender the rest. I am deepening my understanding of what I need to let go of, what doesn't fit with the kind of life I am creating for myself. I am facing the reality that this truth might upset some people. We have to begin to train our minds and hearts not to be validated by a man or the idea of romance to experience love. We must go to the source of the love we desire so that our "cups runneth over." We must be committed to our inner being and the journey of her unfoldment. Not judging her, but observing and allowing the transformation and evolution to happen.

CHAPTER
4

Crawling In Love

W e would all be a lot better off if we just decided to be honest with our fear. We are afraid to give love and afraid to receive it. We are afraid to be vulnerable, afraid the feelings won't be mutual. Afraid of making the first move, afraid that a goodbye might last forever and we will never see that person again.

It is a scary thing to think about falling in love, but what if you decide to crawl in love? I got this idea from a book titled, If the Buddha Dated by Charlotte Kasl, and it changed my perspective of relationship building. It helped my heart to open and release anxiety about the unknowns we face in our love journeys. What if we choose to move with presence and curiosity? What if we moved knowing "I am wonderful with you, and I will be wonderful without you?" Crawling in love has nothing to do with whether that person loves you back. Sometimes the love we desire just is not within the person we desire. They stand just as broken as we, needing just as much healing as we do. What if we saw our love as an act of service to ourselves?

We have to be careful not to get love and romance confused; they are not the same. When I refer to love, I am thinking of the feeling of light, warmth, and safety. That is the love I want to experience in human form. I want us all to know that we are responsible as human beings to do this for each other. Beyond our fears and our limits, we must build the courage to choose love.

> "Owe no one anything, except to love each other, for the one who loves another has fulfilled the law."
>
> ### Romans 13:8

My journey has been inward and I always refer to Matthew 6:33, "But seek ye first the kingdom of God, and his righteousness; and all these things shall be added unto you." My understanding of this is to seek the highest parts of yourself and your potential. Seek your truth, seek yourself and your connection to your higher power, and all things that you desire: peace, bliss, health, wealth, and love will unfold in your life because you have connected to the source from which it evolves.

As I begin to align my mind and heart with God, life flows and happens as an enjoyable experience. I have learned over and over again when you think you are in control, you truly are not, but God is. Centering myself and relying on the power of God has proven itself to be the way for me.

I have learned to use life as a mirror to see what needs to change within me.

I gained this concept of "Life is a Mirror" from practicing Nichiren Buddhism for five years. After my ex-boyfriend survived a skydiving accident, I started seeking the meaning of life and knew there had to be more to it than what I learned in church. I went to get a massage and the massage therapist began to ask me questions about my life. He encouraged me, saying," I tap into the power within to transform my pain, trauma, and family karma." He shared that I had within me the means to become happy no matter what happens in life. I was familiar with Nam-Myoho-Renge-Kyo from my favorite Tina Turner movie, "What's Love Got to Do with It." You can see in the movie how the practice changed her life. I hadn't experienced the kind of abuse Tina had, but the women in my family had: my mom survived abuse from my father, and my great-grand- mother survived abuse from her husband. She had to fight for her life and her children's life. Could you imagine being in the backwoods of the South in the 1950's? There was no one to call for help and if she did call, would anyone answer?

I saw the women in my family go through. I was always aware of red flags and watchful for how a man displays his temper or self-control. I made a promise to myself to never allow abusive behavior in my life. This family karma was going to end! We have to respect each other and we must learn ways to express our true feelings that don't involve physical and emotional harm. We must evolve.

"Despite my promises, I underwent an experience through which I was called to evolve. I could run for ever without facing it, but the time came when I had to face it head-on and accept my karma and consciousness that had manifested. I remember the first day, sitting in the car and feeling frozen in time, asking myself, "How did I end up in an emotionally abusive relationship?" The very thing I had tried to avoid my whole life showed up, and I thought I loved him. I had been in therapy for seven years at this point and was working on myself. I was aware of attachment styles, self-help books, and all of the work that has to be done in this kind of relationship. I felt like I was in the same relationship as my parents. Our arguments escalated over time, then the moment came where I had to decide how I would fight back. How was I going to stand up for myself? Then the evening came where I was afraid someone would get hurt. I yelled for help in an apartment building and some people looked out in the hallway, but just closed their doors. I went outside and asked for help, but people, even the police officer at the red light, said, "There's nothing I can do." At that moment, I felt violated, unsafe, afraid, and unsure of what he was capable of doing. However, I felt very sure of what I could do in defense of myself and that is what scared me the most. I thought of my career, family, and what it would mean to have a record relating to domestic violence. I tried everything to de-escalate, but nothing was working. I felt like no one protects the Black woman.

I am very fortunate in my case because I was never physically hit, but I knew yelling, intimidation, and force are forms of abuse. What would have happened if I stayed? We often normalize toxic behavior: bragging to our friends or family members about who beat who up or "She got me locked up, then bailed me out," throwing clothes out the window then moving back in together. No more! It is time for these cycles of abuse to stop. It is time to heal, it is time to get help related to our triggers and it's time to learn to communicate. Toxic relationships are not okay. I learned in my situation that sometimes you do not know you are in an abusive relationship until you are in one. I learned it could happen to anyone.

This situation led me to dig deep into my fears about men in general. My lack of trust concerning the absence of Black men resulted in a general loss of security within myself and a lack of confidence in men. I told my ex-boyfriend that I felt violated by his behavior: "You are supposed to be my protector if you are the man I love, and if I don't feel safe around you, then where will I feel safe?" Black women have been asking men for year "When will you show up for us, the way we show up for you?" We show up domestically and politically. We show up with an overwhelming responsibility to love you because we know the world wants you dead. It hurts so bad because we know without you, we as a people cannot exist.

After a really bad argument, my father called and gave me direct insight from his experience with abusive behaviour. He talked about being fearful, insecure, and immature. He talked about not having the tools to communicate his feelings and treating women like he owned them instead of loving them. I asked him what I should do. He said, "Most men aren't willing to change. If I were you, I would run." I did not think twice about it. I knew I deserved better treatment and I knew that kind of behavior was a deal-breaker. Either he would take accountability, do his healing and change, or I would not be there to risk arguing, yelling, and feeling unsafe. A lot of this behavior is normal in many domestic partnerships. I knew it was not acceptable for the partnership I wanted for myself.

I wasn't ready to get the wisdom that my relationship's toxicity was a part of my consciousness. Getting that message from an interview held by Kateria Manning with Queen Afua hurt me deeply. I wouldn't say I liked hearing that truth, but it was also liberating to know that my own consciousnesses healing and transformation would be the key factor in transforming my experience. I had to do some deep digging and asking what part of my consciousness was toxic? What part of my being was angry? What part of my consciousness was fearful? I asked, and there it was; toxicity, anger, and fear looking at me in the mirror. I do all the things I am supposed to. How could this be? The answer I received was, "You can run, but you can't hide."

Where we focus our thoughts is what grows in our lives. For example, if my affirmation is, "I don't want a toxic relationship," the universe receives that thought as a prayer for a "TOXIC RELATIONSHIP." So there I was with the exact thing I did not want. The work is transforming the thought and belief to, "I have a happy and healthy relationship where I am safe at all times." The universe captures the feelings and energy of the words HAPPY, HEALTHY, and SAFE. I also re-focused my attention on creating happiness, health, and safety for myself and not relying on another person to provide that for me. Breakthroughs happen when we begin to change our subconscious thoughts and beliefs about ourselves and our lives. We have to realize that our thoughts are prayers and that no prayer goes unanswered.

It says in Matthew 7:7, "Ask, and it shall be given you; seek, and ye shall find; knock, and it shall be opened unto you." I also like what Proverbs 23: 7 says about our thoughts controlling our lives, "As a man thinketh in his heart, so is he." Letting us know we also have a responsibility in our life experience based on our thoughts.

The work to change my thoughts and perception about myself and my circumstances and experiences came through many hours of sitting in meditation, reflecting, journaling and speaking with my therapist and elders.

I told the man I was with that he was toxic and had abusive traits. I told him I could not allow that behavior in my life. That I worked too hard to create a beautiful life to allow anyone in my space that would ruin my peace. That same day he signed up for therapy and committed to getting help. He shared he wasn't aware that his behavior was abusive. That all the couples he knew went through things like this and called it the "motions." I had to have compassion for the man because he learned this behavior was acceptable somewhere along his life journey. Somewhere he had come to believe that this was an expression of love and passion for me and our relationship.

After hearing his perception and more about his own experience, I felt even stronger in my feelings that we are all broken and do not even know it. I felt even stronger that the work we must do as Black people to heal ourselves is more urgent than ever. Perspectives we have been trained to believe and accept culturally have to be destroyed and recreated person by person, family by family. We all know how years of indoctrination and violence have affected the psyche and spirits of our people. Epigenetics proves that the trauma of Anti-Black violence is in our DNA. We have to be more mindful than ever about how violence shows up in our lives and make choices that lead us to love.

While I believe that God made us whole, I believe that things happen in life that begins to break us. If those wounds aren't repaired, we find ourselves in broken situations. The relationship I sought to end forced me to draw closer to God, asking to know the holy spirit even deeper, asking to heal even more, and asking for strength to face my fears and not run from them. Here we GROW again.

Honestly, I had been approaching my life healing journey with a sense of avoidance. I thought that if I avoided the pain, I had healed past it, but it does not quite work like that. You have to face it and be delivered from the pain. If you aren't facing the pain, you aren't growing. Pain is simply a part of life. The point is not to be consumed or addicted to the pain, but to be consumed with healing it and embracing a new feeling.

Before we can love anyone else, we must learn to love ourselves. If we loved ourselves, we would save ourselves from an excess of pain. Most of our days are spent looking outside of ourselves, and we truly must look within. There are no shortcuts: it is an ugly journey, but one that is worth it.

There is nothing more powerful than taking the time to date yourself. Take your time in enjoying new activities and learning what you like and do not like. What are your favorite things about life? What makes you laugh? What do you enjoy doing alone? We often lose ourselves in relationships, and when they are over, we don't know where to begin in rebuilding the connection with ourselves. We often give our power away, time and time again, thinking that doing so is love, but if God is love, why would love take away our power?

If my life-partner showed up today, what kind of person and partner would I be? Many people talk about loving themselves, but it is often just a concept; we do not have a practice in expressing this. One of the practices I had to embrace was saying I love you first thing in the morning. Before I brushed my teeth, did my make up, and got dressed for the day, I would affirm myself and embrace the good and the bad.

One of the most valuable lessons for me has been to discover and embrace my imperfections. To love those parts of myself that still need tenderness, those parts that were maybe unloved as a child and need holding. All relationships are a mirror, and there is a lesson for each of them. Life is all that we know we have for sure. We have no idea, with certainty, what happens when we leave here. When we choose to love ourselves, we don't have to worry about what happens next. We know that because love is the highest vibration and we made the internal choice to connect with that energy, we will land right where we are supposed to be.

"Love Liberates it doesn't bind" - Maya Angelou.

CHAPTER

5

Purpose Mates

We often romanticize relationships that are supposed to be purposeful and spiritual. It is quite easy to get spiritual, soul mate energy confused with romantic sexual energy. There is much value in nonsexual heterosexual friendships. These unions can also assist you with your romantic relationships. How, do you ask? Boundaries! We all need boundaries in our relationships; it's the only way to let people know what they can and can't get away with in a friendship with you. I always say that you are the one to give people permission on how to treat you. It can be hard to have a conversation about boundaries; sometimes, that word itself can be off-putting. So choose more inviting words, something along the lines of, "I want to craft and shape what our relationship is or what our relationship looks like." Then you can start with some guiding questions that allow you both to talk, share, and be heard.

Not being able to set boundaries is one of the reasons people find themselves in breakdowns and fights. All because they were afraid to tell the truth about how they felt. We often hide our feelings and hide our truth to protect the other person, but what makes you think you have the right to decide if the other person needs protection? Maybe what they need is for someone to be honest with them. Someone to push back and hold them accountable.

These relationships can be hard to come by, but I have been fortunate enough to have truth-tellers around me: people who celebrate me and tell me when I am less than my best self. Sometimes their observations come out as jokes or jests, and I do sometimes feel mocked. It is up to me to adjust if I choose without feeling defensive. Trust is an ongoing process. To move closer to the truth, I have learned to ask clarifying questions, a practice that has also been a great resource in strengthening communication and creating foundations for mutual understanding.

I think questions are key to healthy relationships. If you ask questions, you do not have to make assumptions about the other person's intentions. You are allowed to make your decisions from an informed place. You can be clear about yourself, the role you play in the relationship, and what each of you gains in the process.

Purpose mates are those in our lives to help provoke or pull our purpose out of us. We often just live to work, but that is not truly living. We have to enjoy downtime, freedom to explore, create, and allow our purpose to run through us so we can cultivate that gift and share it with the world. The people in our lives who steer us in the right direction are our purpose mates. Sometimes this happens in strange ways. I met someone online who became a good friend and taught me about a plant-based lifestyle, meditation and spiritual books. All of these things are key elements in my life and values now. I made the mistake of thinking the care was romantic, but it was deeper than that: it was sincere and connected to my purpose. The transformation of my life was necessary to fulfill my work in this world, helping others heal by first healing myself. What I was doing to change, empower, and uplift myself became an example of what I would later help others do. That was part of my purpose. I am so thankful for the friend who God assigned to help me fulfill that season's purpose.

We all have a purpose. We are not just here to take up space and waste time. Life goes by fast. We all have a service, an idea, a sown mission inside us. As time passes, that seed is supposed to be watered, and our purpose begins to unfold. The most beautiful thing about discovering the purpose and living in that purpose is you begin to see God provide more than you could ever imagine for yourself. I feel there is no greater joy than pausing for a moment and realizing I could not have created a life like this alone. God created something so wonderful for me.

"God can do exceedingly abundantly above all we ask or think."
Ephesians 3:20

We do not have to search or try to find our purpose mates, just like we do not have to search for our soulmates. They come when your life and your soul are ready. Life is amazing in the way that things work together and come together for your good. You have to remind yourself that all things work together for your good, even in the darkest of days. You are meant to live a happy, fulfilling, and prosperous divine life. You have to wake up, claim your birthright and claim your purpose. The joy is in doing the work to become conscious and find your highest self.

CHAPTER

6

Being Yourself -UNCUT

Choosing to be yourself requires one major thing. You have to discover what that is. You have to do the fear digging and soul searching to decide what parts of yourself you want to keep, what you want to change, and what must go completely. The more digging into yourself you do, the closer to your truest self you can get. Once this space reveals itself, you can never compromise again and return to a lesser version of yourself. You are now held responsible for what you know.

While I was doing this work, I felt extremely isolated. The things that brought me comfort and community were no longer serving this newer version of myself. I liked the aligned version of myself a lot more, but there was not much about societal norms that affirmed consciousness and true happiness, especially for Black women. I had to sit and feel the pain of un-learning and un-doing the version of myself that needed approval, validation from others, and to feel a false sense of security. Sitting alone brought me to face some parts of myself that needed healing and wanted to be free. I was very afraid of what I was going to lose while in this process. I was afraid of the judgment I would get by telling people I didn't desire things that were numbing me. I no longer wanted to be the same person. I wanted my ego, my pain, and attachments to the past to be released and forgiven. I had no idea how to do this, but I would try even if I had to fail.

After a beautiful conversation with a friend about this topic, I discovered this simple idea "How would living in your truth and sharing that truth with someone ever lead you down a path of lack?" We are not responsible for how someone feels after we share our truth. We have to trust that the person is adult and committed enough to their life journey and soul growth to take care of themselves or find the proper outlet or resource to do so. Much of how people respond to us are projections and filled with their limited perspective or own experiences that have nothing to do with us.

I am not saying that you can go around hurting people's feelings, saying anything you want, and being rude. I am saying that you can share that truth with others once you are sure about your truth, having compassion and empathy at the center of the conversation. Most importantly, having compassion for yourself. If you are like me, it is not always easy to discover those feelings or communicate them. That is a process and skill that I am learning to develop. Finding myself in the process of grounding myself, in being uncomfortable yet committed to the process.

"...Compassion towards yourself, you can reconcile all beings of the world."

Lao Tzu.

We have a choice of when and how often we can accommodate our feelings and our truth for the sake of others. I do not think every season of life is like this. I think there are phases, and this is one that is worth exploring for the sake of Self-love. Self-discovery is a beautiful process, and you begin to see everything in the world through a different lens. You begin to release feelings of being attacked or judged or even caring about the opinion of others.

You have to discover your true self, and once you do, you will not ever have to compromise again. This does not mean you will not be tested, because you will. The only way you know who you are is if you are tested. We must try to pass these tests so that we can overcome them and move on. I often sit with myself and ask, "What is it I need to learn?" From there, I make a decision based on what I truly feel God would wants me to do.

I have to be honest; the worst part of this is no longer being able to be petty. We all know the satisfaction and joy of being petty. I was someone who had vindictive behavior. I had to overcome this, and trust me, it is an ongoing process and something I have to practice daily. I still feel like my enemies are lucky. I am trying to evolve this lifetime. Truth be told, there is no greater joy than watching God fight your battles for you.

There is no greater satisfaction than sitting back and enjoying the show. What you put out always comes back; that is just one of the laws of life. Stand up for yourself and know your enemies will be your footstool. All that your enemies are doing helps you to build your character, your strength, and draw closer to spirit. My enemies have been very slick; they have tried to appear as allies and even family. At the same time, trying to destroy me spiritually. Luckily, I have discerned and always prayed that God would reveal my enemies to me, allowing me to cover and protect myself from attacks and spiritual warfare. I have been betrayed; people have tried to control my life and control me with spells and dark magic. Don't be surprised, the bible tells us this will happen, "And the wicked shall be silent in darkness; for by strength shall no man prevail." 1 Samuel 2:9

The plan of the enemy prevailed not. Darkness and evil have tried to follow me, but I have been protected and victorious because of my quest and relationship with God. Chains have been broken.

When I was a little girl, very heavy into the church, I always loved the scripture:

> "For we wrestle not against flesh and blood, but against principalities, against powers, against the rulers of the darkness of this world, against spiritual wickedness in high places."

Ephesians 6:12

I never understood why, and would not understand why until I was well into my adult life and crossed paths with people who did satanic rituals, magic, and sacrifice. The way the enemy works is under camouflage; one of my spiritual advisors told me,

"If the devil showed up with his horns and showing how ugly and dark he is, people would run the other way because they would be scared. The devil shows up very attractive and very cunning and inviting."

I did not know for a long time that I had been exposed to some spiritual darkness. My dreams were strange, my life was not the way I knew it should be, and I knew something was not right.

I was fortunate enough to seek wise counsel and also, that my mother knew the words and power of prayer to bind spirits and demons. In retrospect, going through spiritual warfare is scary only a little because we already know who wins in the end. God gives victory to those who love him. The scary part was trying to keep my mind, while reminding myself that I am not crazy. Reminding myself, I am protected and covered in the blood of Christ. I never in a million years would think that I would share this with anyone. I have asked myself a few times, am I going crazy? Then I would remember that scripture from when I was a little girl, which reminded me God says we would come against battles like this. The great part is knowing the fight is fixed, and we get the victory in the end.

> "But they will not have power over you, for I am with you to take you out of trouble," says the Lord.

Jeremiah 1:19

In life, we experience things we might not want to share with others, to include: sexual, physical and mental abuse, depression and or sadness. Just about any and everything that could cause us to lose our minds! Some of us have been through things that only we ourselves and God knows. We keep quiet to spare the embarrassment, judgment and having to relive our horrors. Although so difficult to bear, these life pains give us our strength and compassion for other human beings. We must love ourselves in order to love others. Love truly is the strongest energy to destroy darkness. If we genuinely loved, there would be no suffering. We walk by and pass suffering each day, feeling powerless in doing nothing about it. Deep down, we all have the answers to overcome and love each other through our suffering. However, we are afraid.

> "But I tell you, love your enemies, bless those who curse you, do good to those who hate you, and pray for those who mistreat you and persecute you."
>
> *Matthew 5:44*

I felt like much of my life was full of self-sacrifice. I felt like I lost myself in the service of others. It took years and many mistakes to find balance in my service to others and service to myself. What good are we to the world if our inner world is unkept and chaotic? I had to learn to be more selfish with my time, energy, and resources. Sometimes people with big hearts have a hard time creating boundaries.

I often wonder why the beginning of anything is so hard. What is the thing that stops us from moving forward or in a new direction? How is that when you make a new decision, sometimes you are faced with problems that takes you back to where you started from?

These problems provoke fear, fear is like adding weight when you are trying to soar. It makes the initial take-off much more difficult. Fear is being still at a green light; all of the pieces are there, even if you can't see them. There are people behind you counting on you going forward so they can get to their destination. There are people watching who are motivated; whose missions are ignited by you fulfilling your mission.

CHAPTER

7

A New Beginning

When I first had the vision for this book, it was based on my desire to start a new life. I had nothing; no car, no apartment, and just a few hundred dollars in the bank to move in with a roommate. Women are trained from a young age to prioritize the needs of the men in their lives. Sometimes that looks like tending to little or big brothers' needs or even supporting Mommy in doing something for Daddy. Black and Brown girls in some societies get called "Mama" as a nickname, but maybe that offers responsibilities a little too soon and limits us from the personal freedom of being a child. This creates issues as we grow into women and find ourselves having a superwoman complex. We devote our energy to driving our careers forward, becoming successful, being beautiful, and being perceived as independent and strong. I have found that this persona is difficult to maintain while also trying to heal and connect with the divine femininity. This creates an expectation that we should embrace our ability to be soft, patient, gentle, and holy. However, we are not given the space to be vulnerable and soft. Some Black girls grow up in environments where being soft and feminine can possibly put them in harmful and violent situations, including sexual abuse. The quality of softness in our community often means vulnerability to harm; it often means weakness. When you are weak or blinded by love, you can potentially get played and hurt. We have watched our mothers be strong, not "put up with no mess," and not need a man for anything. Some of us have adopted the same beliefs.

I had a session with my therapist, where we discussed the need to feel safe and secure and let our guards down. I recalled that the messages I received about keeping myself safe began as early as first grade. In grade school, some of the girls appeared to have been big, loud, and poor. I assumed they were jealous of me. They would threaten to beat me up. From that moment on, I knew I had to protect myself. My uncle, who would pick me up from the bus stop, traveled with a knife, saying, "I gotta watch my back." That was another code engraved in my little mind letting me know I was not safe. Violence is a common part of the Black experience, and fights are sometimes a rite of passage. I had my share of fights and at the core, was the need to defend myself. Most of the time, I was defending myself from the same girls who in grade school didn't like me just because of who I was. I often had issues with more masculine girls. I always stood up for myself, and once they saw I could defend myself, they would fall back.

My point is that rage, anger, and being guarded are responses that keep us in a fearful state; while in this state of fear, we are kept from developing our divine feminine qualities, which are vital when it comes to balancing the world and maintaining relationships.

Independence, aggression, and strength are qualities that Black women often have to embrace to survive. Now it is time for us to thrive. We have to empower ourselves to let go of the toxic coding and lies that this Anti-Black, Anti-Women, Anti-God world has taught us. It is time to return to being graceful. There have to be options in expressing our feminine power outside of being hyper-sexualized and glorified for exposing that sexual energy without anything substantive to gain. The world of pornography, Instagram, Only Fans, etc., have caused some women to become stupefied, giving away their power for a little attention without expecting men to stand up. This world is built on sexual energy, and just like everything else, there is an exchange, a give and take. Oure most powerful gifts as women are our sexuality and ability to give life. Why do we give our gifts away without holding our counterparts accountable in offering their gifts to provide, protect, and love us?

> But if anyone does not provide for his relatives, and especially for members of his household, he has denied the faith and is worse than an unbeliever.
>
> *1 Timothy 5:8*

> Husbands, love your wives and do not be harsh with them.
>
> *Colossians 3:19*

God ordered us to be this way. As long as we are not following the word, we are disobedient; we are out of alignment, and as a result, we are out of balance. I do not stand behind manipulating the word, making it seem as if women are less than men. I am simply saying we all have a role to play.

I felt like I was feminine and could turn on and off my need to be strong and my need to be soft until I was in a relationship that required me to let go and lean into more feminine qualities. I had habits I wasn't even aware of.

As my life played out, I discovered my disconnection with the divine feminine and its qualities. I was shocked! I had to check myself and begin to do the work within.

I started with a fast and detox, journaling, reading the bible and books about relationships and femininity. I danced. I spent time with my mind-body-soul. I dressed up and took my time addressing my traumas and old perceptions of myself, the world, my man, and our relationship. I spoke to friends and women I trusted and leaned on them, knowing that I did not have the answers.

It was taking work, but I was willing to change and stick with an ongoing transformation process. I was willing to transform because I was becoming a better woman. I wanted, and still want, to experience heaven on earth and offer peace and harmony to the world.

It seems as if women are trained by society to look a certain way because it will get them a man. It would appear that this is our ultimate goal in life. However, this false reality is leaving more and more women heartbroken and left feeling empty. We are searching for fulfillment in a place where it does not exist. I had a friend tell me, "Men are simply not capable of our expectations." I didn't want to find the truth in this statement, but if I sit back and look at the facts and receipts of relationships, the proof is there. I do not think it is anyone's fault; I just think both men and women have been taught wrong. We both have false expectations and we are not having honest conversations.

Of course, there are good men. This is not a matter of someone being good or not. This is a matter of expectations and behaviors of men. This is a matter of women being silent when our needs are not met.

In my journey to discover myself outside of a relationship, I tried it all. Club nights with my girls, drinking gin at a bar alone, meeting and dating way too many guys, and falling into rebounds and situations. All of that behavior was me avoiding dealing with my pain and my feelings. I knew that eventually, I would have to begin the real healing process, or I would find myself older, lonely, bitter, and still clubbing and looking for a partner as I crept upon the age of 40 years old. The true journey to begin included a lot of meditation, tears, reading, and love from my friends and mother. I had to grieve and then learn to fall in love with myself again. What we have to give, we can offer to others.

All of this has helped me to rethink my perception and expectations within my relationships. Through my healing, I have attracted empathetic, compassionate, and accountable men willing to address their pain and trauma. Two broken pieces do not create a whole in the context of a relationship. Two whole pieces come together to complete a part of the puzzle of their life.

Men are trained to ignore their pain, but that energy does not go away. It is spewed out of their penis and put into our bodies.

The womb can hold trauma and potentially pass it on to future children. We must learn to be careful with who we share our womb. We can no longer afford to bring children into the world with men who are neither fit nor willing to be fathers.

Our spirit is intuitively seeking those partners and people we made soul promises with to teach, learn, and grow together in earth school. Many thought-leaders have written about the idea that before our souls get to earth, we sign up for the lessons we want to learn and make promises with the people we want to learn from. We tell God what kinds of obstacles we can handle. Once on earth, our life journey is all about unveiling, transcending, and evolving through those obstacles. There is no one to blame: problems are a part of life and overcoming them is part of life's joy.

The more we work on ourselves and see the results of this, the more beautiful and playful life becomes. You begin to laugh at the crazy- crazy things that happen; you begin to see yourself as a co-director. You and God are playing back the story of your life.

Why is it so hard to accept that God loves us and wants the best for us? What are the ways that I choose to struggle, what am I holding onto that causes strife? These are all questions we should ask ourselves. We have to become aware of our thoughts and begin to transform them to change ourselves and society as we know it.

If we can see the results of transformative connection in our daily lives, how can this faith change the pain of poverty and violence in the world? Could it be possible to create a peaceful and just society through consciousness? Could it be possible to know freedom collectively?

Fear and freedom are much closer in their relationship than most think. You cannot have one without the other. You cannot need one if the other is not present in your life. I was afraid of making mistakes, but safety did not get me anything. I thought that living inside the box and "doing the right thing" would lead me to happiness. However, doing the thing that may have infuriated someone is what would have led me closer to my destiny. It has taken me a long time to learn that. It is okay for people not to like you, and it is okay for you to know that not everyone will agree with the decisions you make for yourself.

Mistakes are very necessary, failing is very important, and falling is a unique part of life that allows us to expand in our capacity and learn to walk taller and stronger. You cannot be right all the time. You must be surrounded by wiser people and have experiences that allow you to observe and learn from them.

You must make mistakes, take your losses on the chin, get up, and keep fighting. We must get past the point where we think we are not in the ring in life. Every single day we are in the boxing ring. Some days we are up, the defense is strong, and we have dodged all the jabs thrown our way. Other days while we think we are standing victorious, we catch a quick one-two to the jaw, and we are out for 3, 2, 1. It is just life, always get back up. If we get back up, we are undefeated. Keep your hands up. Love what you love, explore yourself, and explore relationships. When you are ready and decide to embrace your courage to be free, the pieces will begin to fall into place. Eventually, you get to a point where you are no longer judging the experiences as good or bad. You are just experiencing them and taking the lessons for what they are.

Just begin to move your feet and your faith and see where the road will lead you. From my life journey, I know there has been nothing more powerful than choosing TO BEGIN.

CHAPTER

8

Learn As You Grow

I hope aspects of my journey have encouraged you in your own journey. I hope the judgment of your experiences cease and that you feel empowered to know that all things work together for good. No matter how they appear, all things are urging you, pushing or pulling you towards your own divine purpose and soul evolution. Our work is to be conscious of it. Our work is to trust God. Our work is to learn to be. We must trust each moment even when we feel the need to respond outside of ourselves, consciously elevating to our true and highest self. I know it is hard, but it will get easier. The more you ask, the more truth will be revealed to you.

Choosing to heal and to love is what we have all signed up for when we decide to walk a path leading us towards our destiny.

I practice this idea as a mantra. My desire is for my sisters and brothers to know that we are all connected. Everything we do has a ripple effect and response in the universe. My journey is to become self-aware enough at the moment to know when I am causing pain and having enough courage to know when to stop.

My journey includes investing the time, energy, and resources toward having the best possible life experience. My journey is to have the courage to keep walking forward.

All the things that I have shared have not been easy to live through and to feel. I have been sitting in the uncomfortable seat of growth, and although I want to run, I know I cannot hide. I know I cannot get out of this journey without receiving the lessons, doing my work, and keeping my promise to the creator.

Life is full of new chapters and beginnings. We must be aware that we are simply on a journey. Our thoughts and actions determine what that experience will be. We must first fill our cups, carry ourselves with grace, and trust God. This world tries to keep us in a state of confusion and fear, but do not succumb to this state: we must protect our energy, use discernment, and never apologize for walking away from situations and people that do not serve us.

When you walk, you won't be held back; when you run, you won't stumble.

Proverbs 4:12

I am so thankful because I once turned my back against God. I was arrogant, thinking I was in control, but God kept me through all the struggles and never left my side. God always has our backs even when we do not think so.

Even in these moments when it is quiet and we are in the storm an experience of trust arrives. We trust in our knowledge that God hears us and will never leave our sides.

I know all too well what it feels like to not know if God is listening or hearing our calls for help. Again, we have to stay diligent and believe the word is true. "Be strong and courageous. Do not be afraid or terrified because of them, for the Lord your God goes with you; he will never leave you nor forsake you." We can often feel alone, even if others surround us; we often feel misunderstood and judged. This journey is about learning to love and embrace yourself as you are.

"Be brave. Be fearless. You are never alone."

Joshua 1:9

Lean into discovering who you are. The challenge is you might not like who you see, or you may not like the reflection that is looking back at you. I'm not talking about looking in the mirror from a superficial perspective; instead, I'm talking about the reflection of your inner world. You may discover the dark side of yourself. The side that has experienced pain and that has caused others pain. The side you did not even know was you. I was shocked when these aspects of myself were uncovered and flaws began to purge from deep within. During this time trusting others was out of the question. I knew I could rely on myself, but the possibility of relying on others was way too scary for me. It was uncomfortable, but if I did not overcome this challenge, I knew it would leave me alone and without the love relationship I truly desired.

I think that our life work is to learn to open our hearts. Life experiences bruise our hearts and sometimes create what may feel like holes or voids. Our work is to learn to repair what has been broken. To know we have the power to transform our experience.

I have been fortunate enough to have spent the last few years soul searching and working on my subconscious mind. I pray and meditate before I go to sleep, in the middle of the night around 4 am, and when I wake up. I thought this process was supposed to make me feel better, but it was isolating, lonely, and raw. I came to know where I was and where I wanted to go: I was trying to dive deep to break patterns, behaviors, and generational habits. In this journey, I had to go through the mud.

A spiritual journey is about awakening your higher purpose and coming to know that God had your back no matter what. It is about coming to know that

40

all things are one and all things work together for good through your conscious evolution.

Many of us do not know where we are going or how we are going to get there. Part of the process is becoming aware that we create where we are going with our thoughts and the actions we take each day, each week, each month, each year, each decade, creating the life we will leave behind when it is all done.

Starting a journey is never easy. Sometimes, we do not know where to start, but all you have to do is stand where you are and take one step. Each step will lead you closer to your final destination. I encourage you to make your vow to begin to love yourself more, with self-care rituals and routines, goals centered on your mental, physical, and emotional health, and on honoring your physical health for the best quality of life possible.

This part of my journey in self-love and healing ends with contentment. It ends with an awareness of the ups and downs, the ebbs and the flows, and pride that I DID IT! I loved myself enough to fully embrace me. I loved myself enough to be dedicated to healing. I loved myself enough to forgive. I loved myself enough to set myself free from fear, doubt, worry, depression, and anxiety. Society works hard to keep us fearfully living out our insecurities. We must work even harder to guard our minds and hearts and be connected to the one thing that truly matters the most, love.

I thought all of this would be easy to express, but in the heat of anger, betrayal, fear, and arguments, love can be the last thing you think about. It is in these situations that you need to love the most. We need love in the world more than ever, which means we need to focus on loving ourselves more than ever so that we have cultivated enough love to give. Women are the healers of the world. We deserve the time, space, and resources, to be in a state of peace and to align with God so we can heal ourselves and our loved ones. We must step into our power and our divine nature to balance the world.

Our outer lives are a reflection of our inner lives. Whatever you see in your environment is what is within you, waiting to change, and waiting to be unleashed. I wish I could tell you that the journey to your divine nature will come easily, but it will not. You have to learn to accept the journey for what it is and constantly transform your thoughts. Simultaneously, you must relax and enjoy the process: allowing God to do what he does best.

I do not have all the answers, and I am learning as I go. I know that dedicating my time and energy to healing myself, doing the work, and growing closer with God is the best journey. We cannot always numb our pain because numbing welcomes disease and disharmony. There are enough people who strategically work to inject that into the world. We must work even harder to keep ourselves healed and aligned. Through meditation, prayer, therapy, proper diet, and a healthy relationship with yourself, a healthy relationship with others unfolds. You must build such a state of security within yourself; then others will know how to respect you, and those that do not are given boundaries and no longer have access to you.

There was a period where I was tested. I had to decide to stand alone rather than be in relationships and friendships that did not honor and respect who I was becoming. Sometimes people do not want the new version of you. It can be too much of a challenge for them to step up to the standards that your life is now requiring.

CHAPTER

9

Hear You, Loud and Clear

There is one thing I feel so clear about after going through the ups and downs of relationships and trying to build a more authentic and truthful relationship with my inner voice. I am learning that relationships can place us on the path we need to be on to come into the true depths of who we are.

Many of us have sacrificed ourselves for love relationships with men way too many times. I made a vow in my life that the generations of women who self-sacrifice for anyone ends with me.

The more I try to focus on loving myself and increasing my self-worth, the more I am in partnership with myself and preparing for a partner who exudes the same. We have to take ourselves out of a victim state no matter what the other person did wrong. We attract the person and the circumstances. It is a hard truth to accept, but we must accept this to change and make different choices. That is the whole point of being empowered: activating your power no matter what and deciding that you will win, overcome, and learn the lesson. There is only one true relationship, which is becoming one with the living God and your inner self.

Without God, where would I be? Without knowing that the energy dwelling in the heavens also resides in my soul, where would I be? Every day I work to clean up my inner life and refine the voice that I know as my intuition. Your intuition will never lead you in the wrong direction. You must trust, be obedient and know, come what may, that you can always start again as long as you don't give up. New beginnings allow life to give you something greater than you could ever imagine. You do not have to know where you are going; all you must do is move.

I am ending this section of my journey, sort of where I started, at the end of a relationship that brought about the vision and impulse to reach within to see what I could find.

As I am coming to the close of this book and closing this part of my journey, I feel confident in saying to Black Women that it is our responsibility to love and care for ourselves. This world is not going to do it, so we should stop asking and waiting. I have tried so many alternative spiritual paths over the years, trying to accelerate my desire for life; as I mentioned before, I turned to Buddhism and chanting Nam-Myoho-Renge-Kyo, Crystals, Sage, divination, and spiritual rituals. I had spiritual work done, too. While some of it may have worked with different challenges, none of it delivered me. None of it wiped away the kind of inner pain I felt and wanted to break away from. I got further away from God even though I was truly seeking Him all along.

At one point, I felt proud to be taking another route in my spiritual path, but life humbled me, and I had to come to learn the power of Christ. All those alternative practices were getting me by, they felt good and empowering–but my life was not moving the way that I knew it should. I knew in my spirit that my blessings and internal connection were not in the right place. I feel grateful now because I know that I was only brought out and exposed in order to have a testimony.

It took me fearing for the wellbeing of my life and a sociopathic man to wake me up. My back was against the wall. I was in debt, scared, confused, and alone. I was backed into a corner where I had no choice but to call on the mighty name of Jesus to help save my mind and restore my life.

My life was truly a mess. On the outside, I was still beautiful, in shape, and doing my work to inspire and motivate others, but who motivates the motivator? My own inner life was struggling. I did not feel like I could talk to anyone because I was ashamed and embarrassed. God had allowed circumstances in my life to break me down so that he could rebuild me. I had no strength, and I turned to the word of God to find comfort and peace during my storm. I started to seek scripture.

Many times, emotions took over my logic and it took way too long for me to listen to my inner voice. The gut never lies. When we don't listen to our gut, our lives lead to a dark place. A place so dark, only God's grace, mercy, and love can bring us out. When I was in the midst of my storm, I felt so low that some days I couldn't get out of bed. Then I would feel so bad that I would cry because there was not a safe space to share all the emotions.

It took some time, but eventually, I did get my strength and got out of bed. I made it to the floor at midnight to pray for healing. I had to remind myself who loves me. If I could just stop seeking what is God's unconditional love from others, then I would be straight. I would have all aspects of my life in order. However, that is not the case with most of us. We want that love from a man.

I have been searching for myself for a long time, but I did not have to search far. My true self was there all along. The true self was made in the image and likeness of God. The true self says I am a child of the King.

"Before I formed you in your mother's womb, I knew you."

Jeremiah 1:5

45

The best of who we are already reside within, we simply need an unveiling of that identity.

The most important lesson my soul has been trying to learn is to listen to the inner guidance led by God's voice. I tried to do it my way repeatedly, and each time I failed. I wonder what would happen if we raised our perspective to that of heaven. I have learned that we do not have to seek to find something that God has already placed inside of us. The pains and the world's trauma have made us believe that we aren't already embodied expressions of love, but we truly are. We are love because God is love, and we are made in the image and likeness of God. We possess the very same love God has for us.

This journey is about denouncing and rejecting the lies the world tells us. The world tells us repeatedly how imperfect we are, but the word tells us that, "We may be perfect, complete, and lacking nothing." Loving ourselves is a birthright, yet this world has made it so hard for us to love ourselves the way we are. It has projected so many images towards us that affirm we have to change and that we are not good enough. What if we did not feel the need to get surgery or find ways to change how God created us. I truly believe loving yourself in the most natural state is one of the first steps in fully embracing ourselves and coming into a deeper sense of self-knowing. I think we all spend a lot of time trying to know and understand someone else's inner workings, especially in our love relationships. If you don't understand yourself, how can you grow to know anyone else?

Our journeys have more in common than we think. Wherever you are in your life, you and God have the power to create the best of it. You have the power to let go and trust the process. I had to learn to trust my pain. I had to accept that no one ever told me that life wouldn't challenge me. The older I get, the more challenging the obstacles become, but the challenges also draw me into my divine purpose and relationship to God.

I have had to accept that learning to love and honor myself as a fearfully and wonderfully made daughter of God, is the liberation I have been seeking from men. My biological father cannot give me the feeling of safety and joy that I truly desire, and no man can give me what I am seeking to complete myself. I encourage everyone to take the time to reflect and decide that it is okay if you do not know where you are going.

All you must do is begin.

Father God, Your love oh God will pierce through the lies of the enemy and what he has told us in our night seasons. Father flood us with your presence... make your love so tangible that it can't be denied. Blow your Holy Spirit power over our mind, body, and soul. That every hidden thing, broken parts of us will be mended. Amen.

CHAPTER

10

Doing the Work

When did I start
betraying myself?

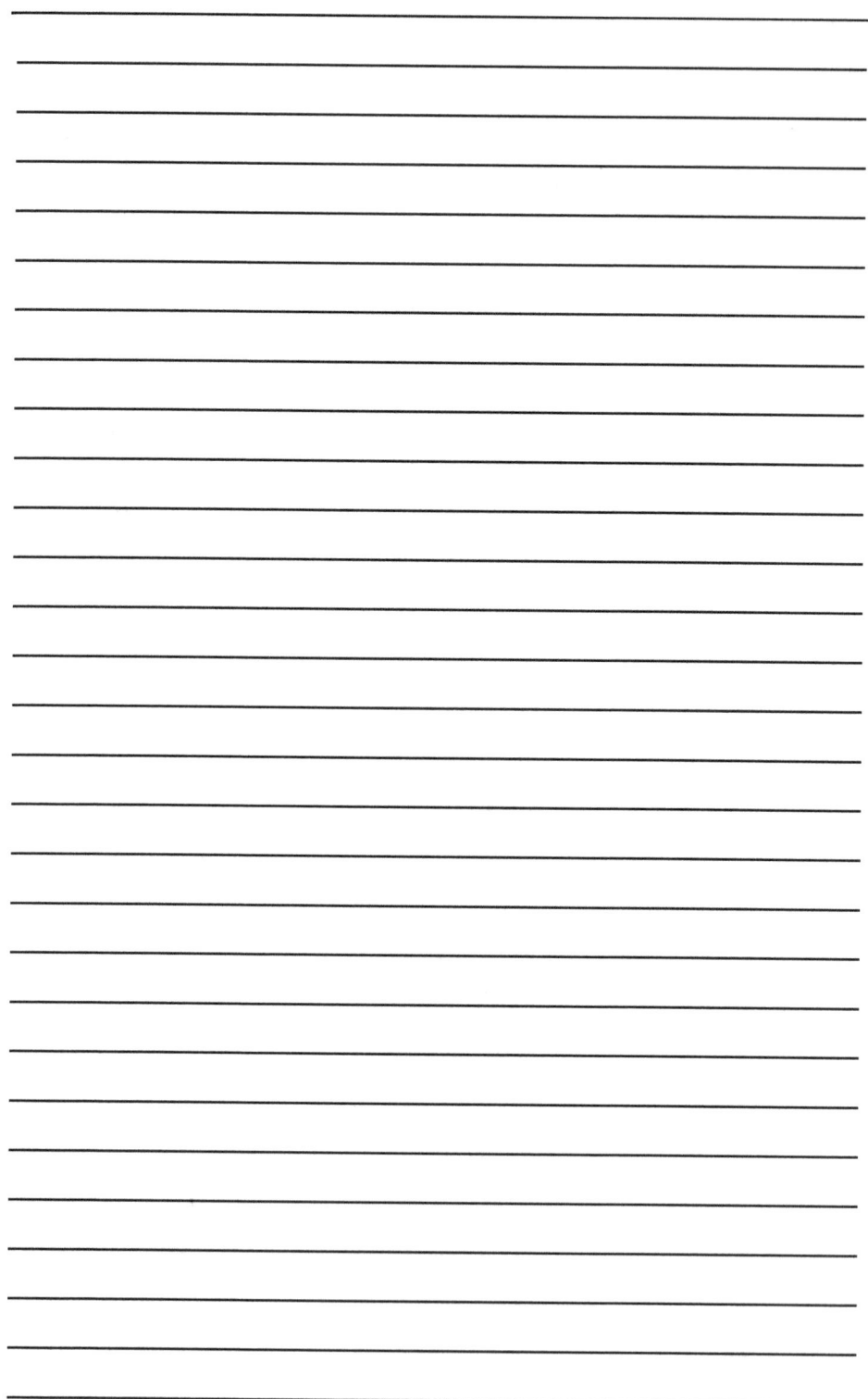

Where was I in my life
when I welcomed betrayal?

What is it that I'm truly seeking?

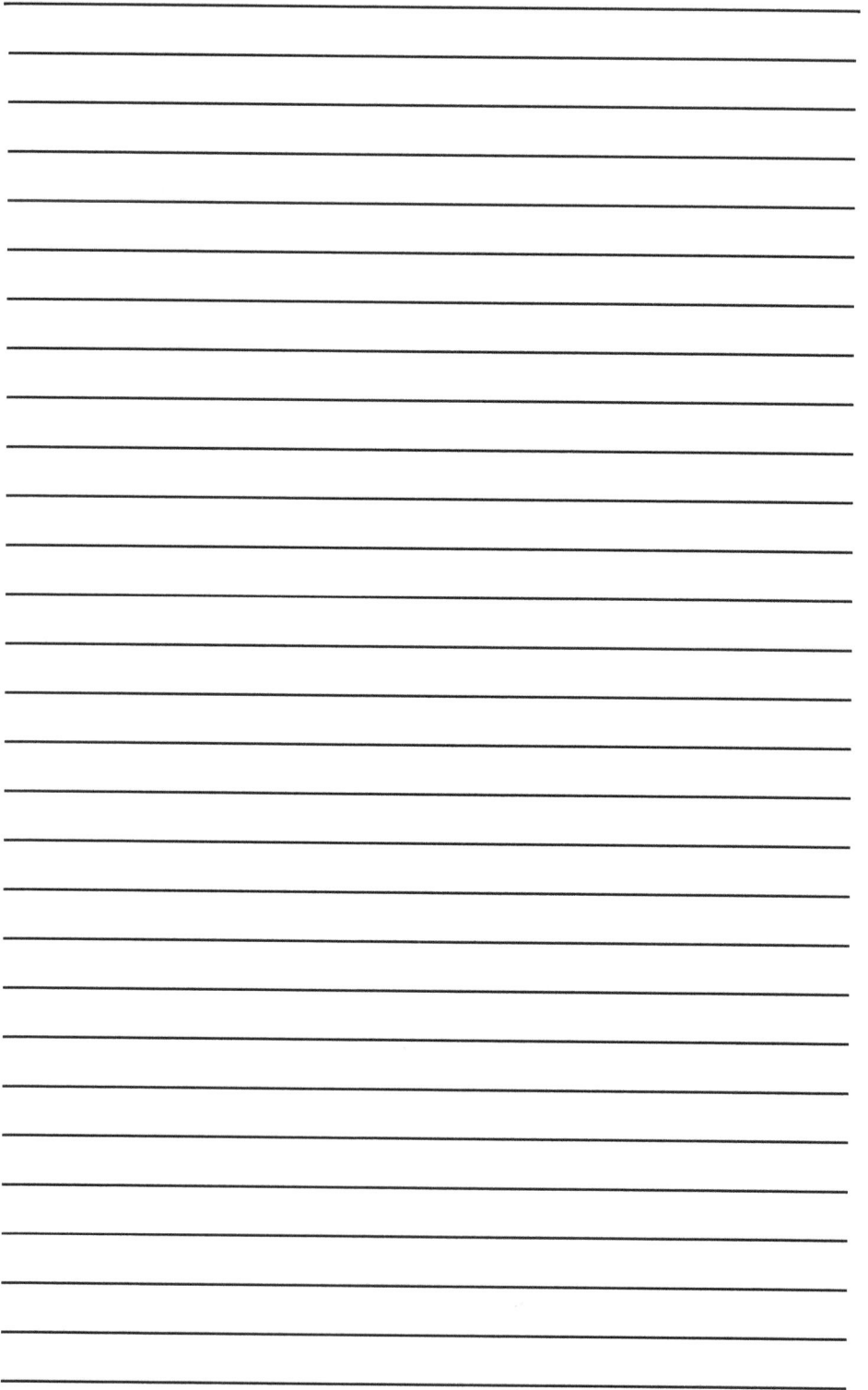

Who do I need to forgive
in order to learn love ?

How do I want to experience love in my life?

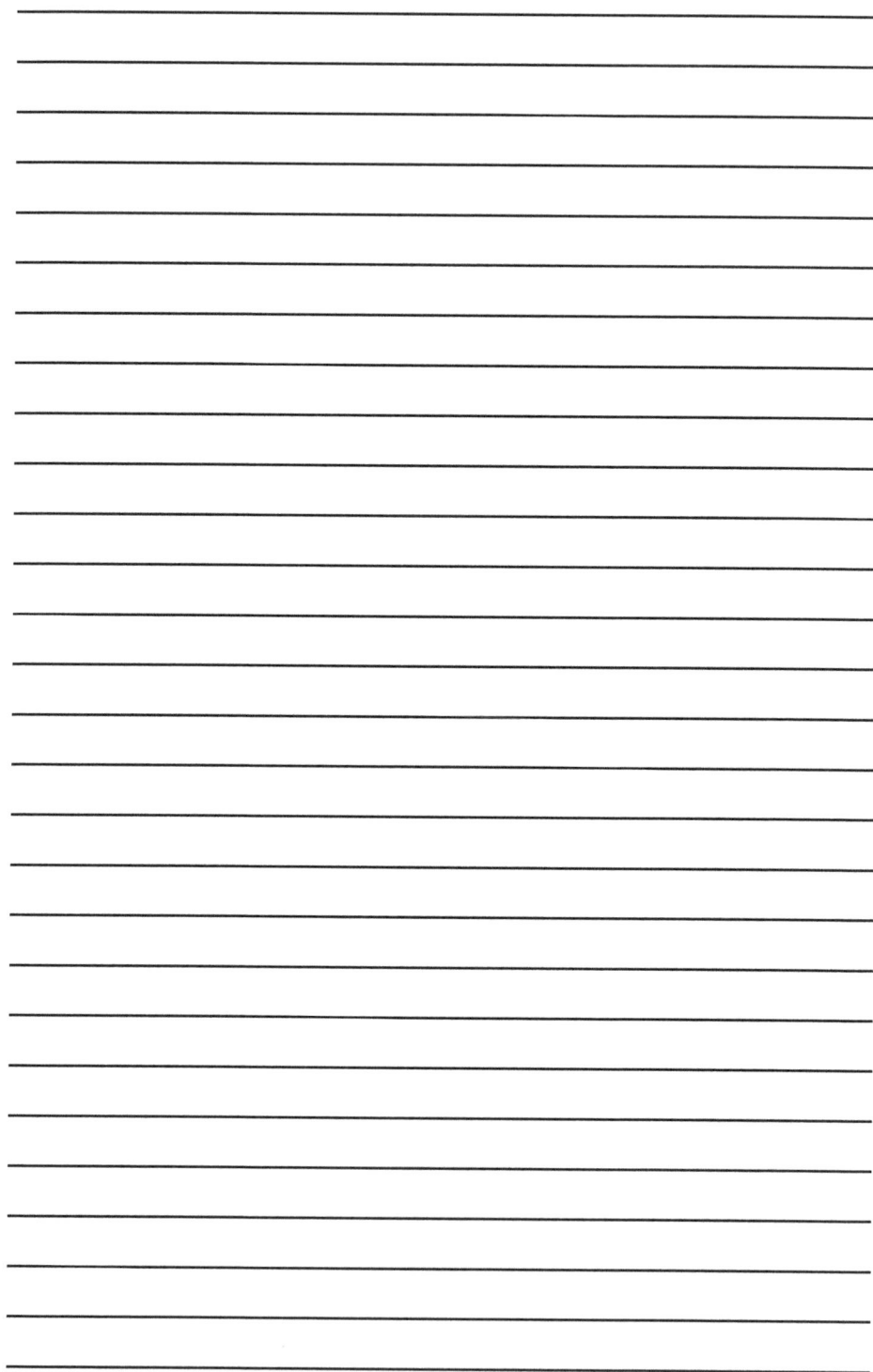

What are the things that make me feel a sense of peace and happiness ?

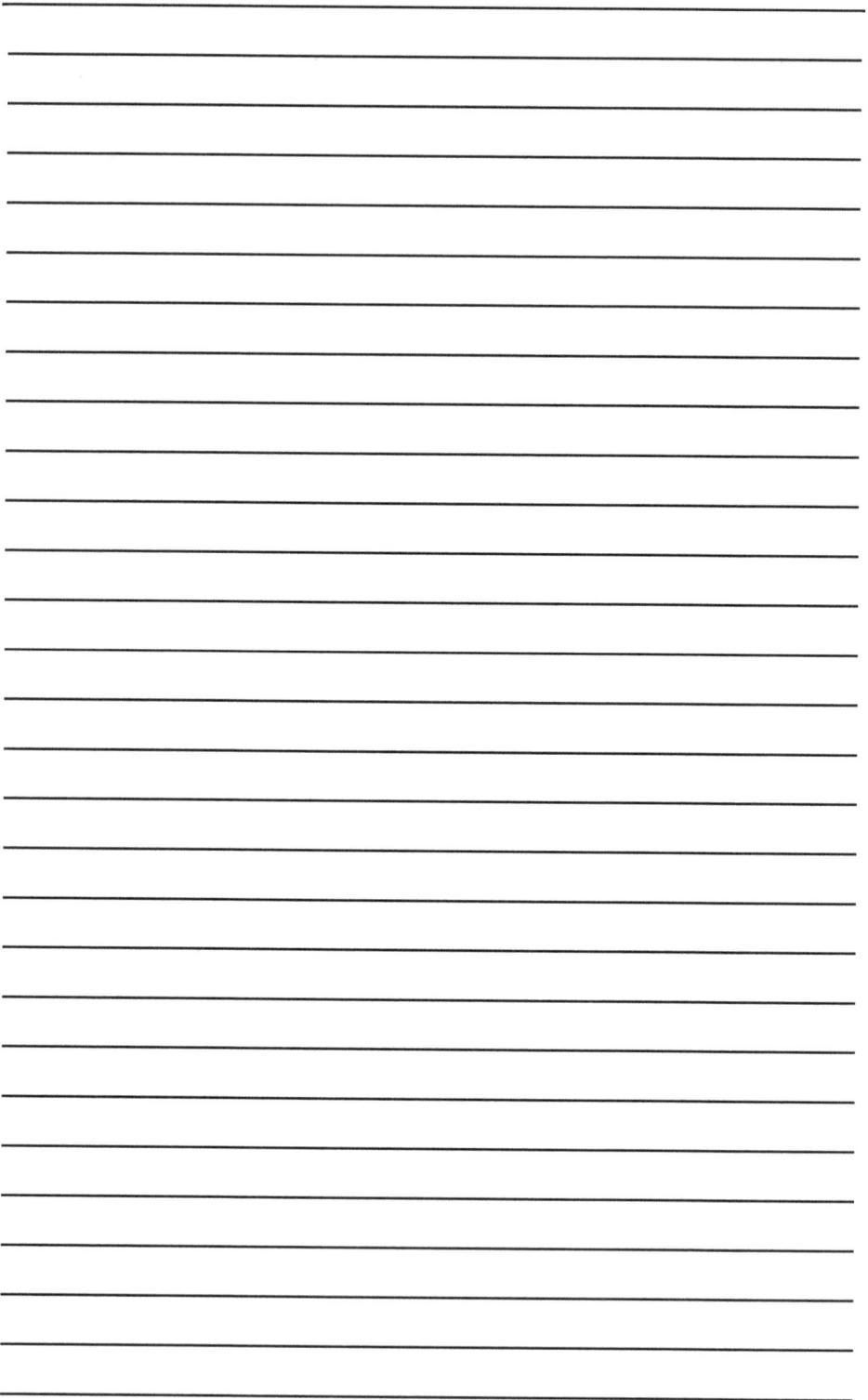

If No didn't exist what kind of life would I be living?

If I walked into my purpose
where would it lead me ?

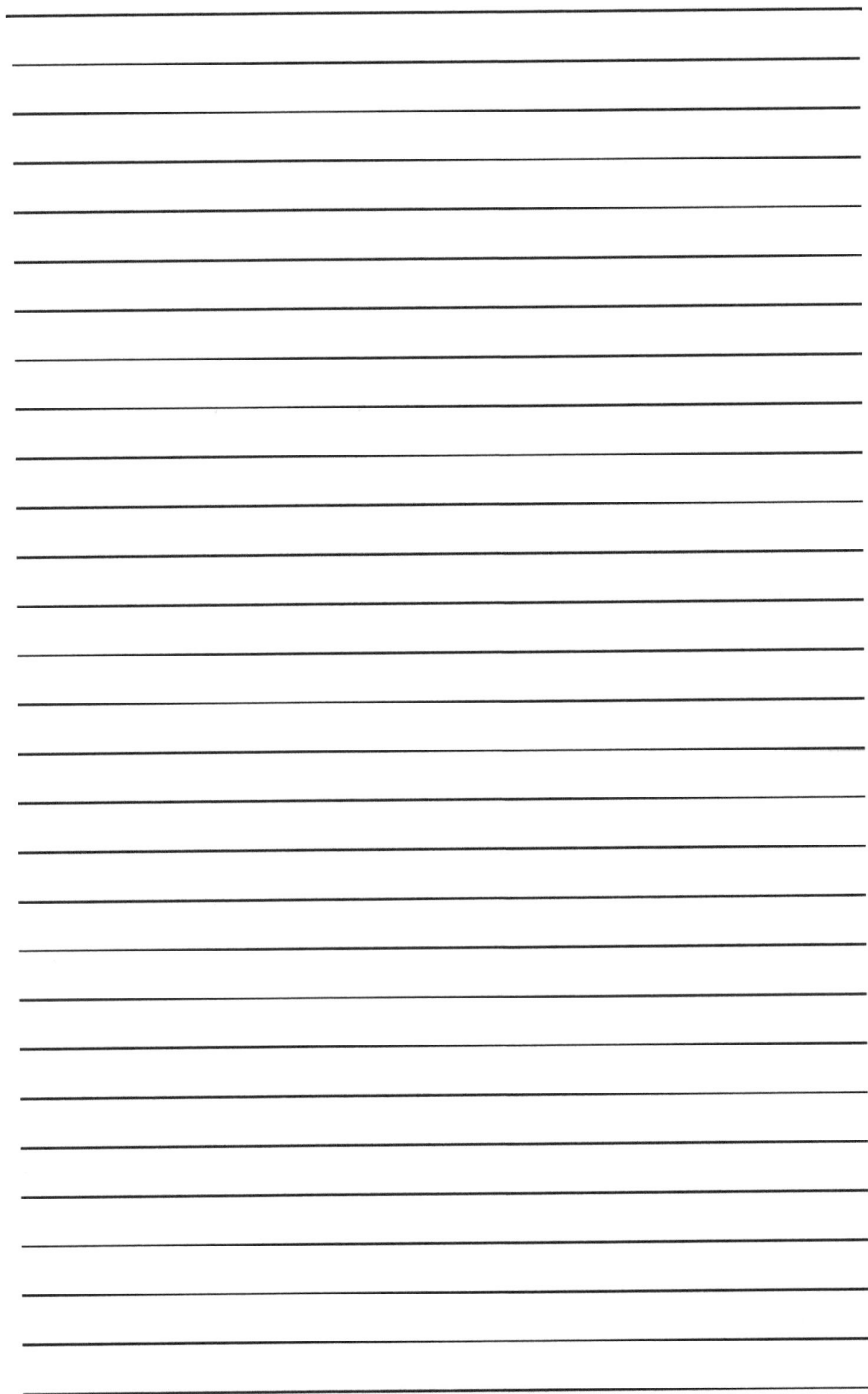

What do I have to surrender in order to step into my new beginning?

Write a letter to your future self thanking her for the courage to start again and expressing gratitude for her transformation.

ABOUT THE AUTHOR

Sakina Ibrahim is a woman who knows the value she brings to the table and is not afraid to write about it. Her unique style has earned her an NAACP Image Award nomination for her publication "Big Words To Little Me." Sakina has spent over a decade studying and teaching dance all over the world, which has provided her an unparalleled experience of the arts. She has commanded the eye and ear of Drexel University, George Washington University, University of California Irvine, the Boston Women's Conference, Michigan State University, The Trayvon Martin Foundation, and The Annual Essence Festival.

Specializing in Diversity, Inclusion, and Equality drove her to offer free online courses such as "Becoming Your Best Self" and launch her podcast *Quest for Truth* - A place for inspiring conversations about spirituality, art, and culture. An entrepreneur at heart, Sakina has stepped out on her own and started her own wellness company, "Stretch and Pray." Stretch and Pray focuses on being emotionally, physically, and spiritually balanced. Sakina continues to expand her passion for the arts, creativity, and healing nationally through classes, workshops, speaking engagements, and film. Look out for the launch of her nonprofit "Global Girl" in 2021.

Find out more at http://www.sakinaibrahim.com/